Cries Behind Lies:

Domestic Violence an Imposter in the Church

PALMETTO
PUBLISHING
Charleston, SC
www.PalmettoPublishing.com

Copyright © 2024 by Cheryl C. Prescott

All rights reserved
No portion of this book may be reproduced, stored in a retrieval system, or transmitted in any form by any means—electronic, mechanical, photocopy, recording, or other—except for brief quotations in printed reviews, without prior permission of the author.

Paperback ISBN: 9798822962972

Cheryl C. Prescott

Cries Behind Lies:
Domestic Violence an Imposter in the Church

Thank you for purchasing Cries behind Lies. God of all people may the essence of our hearts respect other faith and traditions I offer you peace, I offer you love, I see beauty in all of us, may our wisdom flow from the brightest source, may peace bestow on us all.

Love and Blessing, Cheryl C. Prescott

To My Beloved Audience,

As you begin reading this book, you will notice there are no chapters, only subtitles. The numbering system is not included on the pages because I want the eyes to capture the anonymous embrace of what you are reading. It is a good read to stimulate the soul, heal the mind and commit to the entire reading. No need to look for chapters it distracts the thought process like a whirlwind. Enrich your body, mind and soul as you journey into Cries behind Lies an imposter in the church, and how you too can be a vehicle in heightening awareness. A word of encourage to my survivors and those who are still entrapped. Be brave, fight for what you believe in by utilizing your God given innate ability, there will be obstacles, defeats, and hardship but you will always win if you persist. Trust in the Lord, be strong and courageous it's already done.
Cheryl C. Prescott

Special thanks and Acknowledgement.

I am forever grateful for my grandmother Thelma Prescott and my mother Annette Prescott who was survivors of domestic violence and were strong in the Lord, never gave up in the fight against domestic violence. To my only daughter Karisma Prescott, love you. Thank you for always supporting my work in fighting domestic violence and always be there for me. Abria, Azja, and Azaria thank you for the laughter, and fun filled family vacations and our family dog Zoey.

To the President of the United States of American, President Joseph R. Biden, thank you as Senator you introduced the H.R. 3514 Violence Against Women Act, and on September 13, 1994, the landmark VAWA was signed into law. President Biden shared that the VAWA is his proudest legislative accomplishment and "No one deserve to be abused and no woman should blame themselves." **President Joseph R. Biden.**

To my spiritual father, Dr. A.R. Bernard who encouraged me to be persistent and determined in all that I set my mind to do, and because of you; I wrote the book. Thank you.

To Professor Douglas Thomas my college professor, who prayed with me in my darkest moments always inspiring me to excel.

To Pastor Brown due to your leadership and spiritual teaching at Christian International Outreach Ministry, I became an ordained minister.

To Mr. Lenny Green, WBLS night radio host, thank you for supporting those who experience domestic violence and bringing awareness to your radio audience.

To everyone who has prayed for me and came into my life for a reason, season, or lifetime I am forever grateful and express my love and appreciation by saying Thank you.

A very special Thank you to all the staff at Palmetto Publishing you are amazing.

How Ancient Laws Ruled.

In the beginning, God created the heavens and the earth. The creator did not create domestic violence, so where did domestic violence originates and begin? We will explore English common Law that affected women's lives leading to domestic violence and how faith leaders can educate the flock.

753 B.C. During the reign of Romulus in Rome, wife beating is accepted and condoned under The Laws of Chastisement. Under these laws, the husband has absolute rights to physically disciple his wife. By law, a husband is held liable for crimes committed by his wife, this law was designed to protect the husband from harm caused by the wife's actions. These laws permit the husband to beat his wife with a rod or switch if its circumference is no greater than the girth of the base of the man's right thumb, as we know it to be The Rule of Thumb. These laws are perpetuated in English Common Law and throughout most of Europe.

202 B.C. At the end of the Punic Wars, the family structure changes giving women more freedoms, including property rights and the right to sue their husbands for unjustified beatings, however, the

Church fathers re-established the husband's patriarchal authority and the patriarchal values of Roman and Jewish law. The Roman Emperor, Constantine the Great, had his wife burned alive when she is no longer of use to him. In Europe, noblemen beat their wives regularly. The Church sanctions the subjection of women. Priests advise abused wives to win their husbands good will through increase devotion and obedience. **In medieval theological manual**, a man is given permission to castigate his wife and beat her for correction.

1400's The Christian Church vacillated between support of wife beating and encouraging husbands to be more. compassionate and use moderation in their punishments of their wives. **A medieval Christian scholar**, Friar Cherubini writes. the Rules of Marriage, in support of wife beating.

1427 A Christian Minister in the Church suggests that his male parishioners exercise a little restraint and treat their wives with respect, but no one listened. Lord Hale, an English Jurist, who sets the tradition of non-recognition of marital rape. Hale states that when women married, they gave themselves to their husbands in contract and that contract could not be broken our withdrawal until they divorced. Lord Hale was characterized as a misogynist who burned women at the stake as witches and these laws permitted and allowed women to be burned and buried alive.

1500's Early settlers in America utilized the Old English Common Laws that explicitly permits wife beating for correctional purposes. **In 1792** Mary Wollstonecraft in a vindication of the Rights for

Women seeks changes in the education for women and respectable treatment by husbands.

1824 The decision by the Mississippi Supreme Court in Bradley v. State of Mississippi Walker allows a husband to administer only moderate chastisement in case of emergency.

1829 In England, a husband's absolute power of chastisement is abolished. Francis Power Cobbe publishes articles on Wife Torture in England. Cobbe denounces the treatment of wives in England in which she documents 6,000 of the most brutal assaults on women over a 3-year period who had been maimed, blinded, trampled, burned and murdered. Francis Power Cobbe presents a theory that abuse continues because of the belief that a man's wife is his property. Due to her document long fight the Matrimonial Causes Act is passed in 1878 allowing victims of domestic violence to obtain legal separation from the husbands, entitles women to custody of their children, and to retain earnings secured during the separation. These Act many sound good but there were many stipulations just as with the VAWA.

The Matrimonial Causes Act of 1878 separation order could only be obtained if the husband has been convicted of aggravated assault and the court consider her in grave danger. As with Queen Victoria ascension to the Throne, lawmakers begin enacting reforms regarding women. Wives were no longer kept under lock and key, life threatening beating were considered grounds for divorce and wives couldn't be sold into prostitution.

1911 The first Family Court is created in Buffalo, NY. Professionals believed that domestic violence courts will better solve family problems in a setting of discussion and reconciliation engineered by social service intervention. This was the beginning of the systematic official diversion and exclusion of violence against wives from the criminal justice system. Fifty-one years later in 1962 in New York City, <u>domestic violence cases are transferred from Criminal Court to</u> <u>Family Court where only civil procedures apply</u>. The abusers never faces the harsher penalties as like today when found guilty in Criminal Court for assaulting his wife or girlfriend. We have only touched the surface of how English Common Laws were highly considered in marital and intimate partner relationships. In a study and research conducted by Minnesota DSM men were always given the male honor to do whatever they want to their wife. This bring us to the start of the 1970's

Feminist Movement.

The feminist movement emphasizes egalitarianism and participatory organizational models. Women were inspired and sustained by their relationships with others, by knowing that their work to end domestic violence is crucial. We have come a long way from Congress passes laws prohibiting discrimination against women in employment and requiring equal pay for equal work, Maine opening of the first shelters in the United States, and the development of the women's rights feminism and liberation movement providing hotlines and crisis center for battered women to speak out and seek help. In the last 30 years Domestic Violence movement has accomplished an enormous strength of courage. In 1987 this marks the first Domestic Violence Awareness Month held in October 1992

The American Medical Association and the United States Surgeon General suggested that all women patients be screened for domestic abuse, 1994 The U.S. congress passed the Violence against Women Act as we know of today the VAWA as part of the federal crime bill. VAWA funded services for victims of domestic violence, rape, provided training to increase police and court officials' sensitivity to domestic violence. $1.6 billion was authorized for the years of 1994 to 2000.

Domestic violence is draconian, a pattern of abusive behaviors in the form of physical, sexual, emotional, financial and any cruel behavior used by one partner of an intimate relationship to control their partner and maintain power in the relationship. **Domestic violence** crosses all ethnic, racial, socioeconomic, and sexual orientation boundaries.

Why this book?

Cries *Behind Lies* is not a fix- me up book or a psychological approach to understanding domestic violence. This book is written for any reader to reach beyond the wounds, hurt, and fears during times when others hurt them through domestic violence behavioral acts. This is no attack on any religion or faith-based communities, or on men. This is about cries behind lies domestic violence as an imposter in the church and the people who face brokenness and looks toward the church for help, but sadly enough, the church is masked and cunningly disguised by an ecumenical word. Survivors, by God's grace, can walk in the light that was once surrounded by demonic darkness. As you continue to read the Colophon it highlights how pastors and faith leaders can truly open their congregations to those who rely on the biggest institution for help. Revictimization is what happens when a woman or mean leaves their abuser to come to their place of worship and return to the abuser. Chiefly speaking victims sit in the churches, listen to the sermon, but never have the instructing biblical text, or prayer assuring them that we believe your story and asking how we can help you to heal in this journey.

In the book of Psalm chapter 11 verse 5 "The Lord tests the righteous but the wicked and him that loveth violence his soul hate."

The Narrative

In the beginning God created the heavens and the earth and the earth was without form and void: and darkness was upon the face of the deep. And the Spirit of God moved upon the face of the waters. And God said. Let there be light; and there was light, and God saw the light that it was good, and God divided the light from the darkness. And God called the light day and the darkness night and evening and the morning were the first day. And God said, Let there be a firmament in the midst of the waters, and let it divide the waters from the waters, and God mad the firmament divided the waters which were under the firmament from the water and called the firmament Heaven and the evening and morning was the second day. The God saw everything that he had made was very good, heavens and the earth and all the host of them were finished. The Lord God formed man of the dust of the ground and breathed into his nostrils the breath of life and man became a living being. The Lord God planted a garden eastward in Eden, and there he put the man whom he had formed, and the Lord God said, "It is not good that man should be alone" I the Lord will make him a helper comparable to him." The Lord God caused a deep sleep to fall on Adam, and he slept, and he took one of Adam ribs and closed the flesh in its place. Then the rib which the Lord God had taken from Adam he made into a woman. Adam said, "This is now bone of my bones and flesh of my flesh, she shall be called Woman because she was taken out of man". And it came to pass, when men began to multiply on the face of the earth and daughters were born unto them, that the sons of God saw the daughters of men that they were fair, and they took them wives of all which they chose. And the Lord said my spirit shall not always strive with man, for that he also is flesh yet his days shall be a hundred and twenty years. There were giants in the earth in those days and after that, when the sons of God came in unto the daughters of men and they bare children to them, the same became might men which were of old men. And God was that the wickedness of man was great in the earth, and that every imagination of the thoughts of men's heart was only evil continually. And it repented the Lord that he had mad man on the earth, and it grieved God at his heart. An the Lord said, I will destroy man whom I have created from the face of the earth. But Noah found grace in the eyes of the Lord. These are the generation of Noah, Noah was a just man and perfect in his generation, and Noah walked with God and Noah begat three sons, Shem, Ham, and Japheth. And the Lord saw that the earth was corrupt and filled with violence. The biblical book of Genesis begins with the creation of God who never intended his earth to be violentor corrupted. The book of ***Genesis 6:13*** "Then God said to Noah, read it."**In the book of 2 Samuel chapter 13 verses 1-22 the** writer captures a biblical story of Tamar King David daughter who is virgin and is raped by her half- brother Amon when King David heard the news he was angry but refuse to address his son because King David love Amon his oldest child. This is the first violation of a woman in the bible and even King David a man after God own heart refuses to address the rape of his daughter. Unfolding the true at times is difficult to grasp, we embrace these stories to know that the Lord is still on the Throne and despite facing many challenges in life he will see us through. Stay prayed up, strong and courageous in the Lord.

Religious leaders of Ezekiel's Day

Ezekiel's Day were criticized by Jesus. Read Ezekiel chapter 43 verse 3.Jesus stated and you experts in the law woe to you because you load people down with burdens they can hardly carry, and your religious leaders will not lift one finger to help them.My beloved, there are many burden down in the church who are hopeless, and beaten down, asked yourself how can we help them. The book of **2 Samuel 22: 3** "My God, my rock, in whom I take refuge." read it.

Jane's Story

It is 8 pm Jane Doe is overwhelmed with pain and fear, sitting at the kitchen table with every bone in her body aching, face bruised her eye black and blue swollen shut, her husband had just stormed off in his car after another family outbreak as he calls it, feeling trapped with no idea where to turn, Jane reaches out to call the pastor of the church she sometimes attends,Imagine that you are Jane's pastor What would you do?

Sam's Story

It was 6:30 pm and Sam a tall 6 feet 9 self-employed business owner returned home and as always dinner is unprepared, he asked his wife, honey will you like to order out, Sam's wife started name calling and expressed you should have gotten dinner on your way in. Sam is optimistic about making his marriage work, but pessimistic if he should stay in the marriage, or reach out to his pastor about what is going on the household.

<u>Rebuilding</u>

Domestic violence is shattering lives in one or more families in your church. **Domestic violence is one of the secret tragedies occurring within the church. In a predictable progression of events that seems to continually repeat itself in an abusive relationship.** In the abusive relationship the *first phase* is a time of tension building, and irritations over things like finances. Regardless of the victim's efforts to avoid confrontation the crisis phase is inevitable.

The second phase starts when acute violence begins, this is when the batterer unleashes their aggressive behavior on their partner. The abuse can be verbal or physical. After the explosive release of violence, a period of relative calm follows, this is the remorse phase, like a penitent alcoholic, the abuser may express guilt, show kindness and remorse, shower his or her partner with gifts and promise that the violence will never happen again. Their behavior often comes from a genuine sense of guilt over the harm he or she inflicted, as well as the fear of losing their spouse. The significant other may really believe they never allow himself or herself to be violent again. The victim wants to believe their partner and for a time, may renew their hope in the ability to change. The problem is that the cycle will repeat itself unless outside intervention takes place and the victim is ready to leave their abuser. Reader, what can all of us do on our part to take inventory of a domestic violence situation? for one we can ask questions about their abuser, like, does the abuser continually monitor your time and make you account for every minute when you are out or visiting friends.? Do you every feel isolated and alone, as if there were is no one with whom you could confide? Is the abuser overly critical of daily things, such as your cooking, clothes, or appearance? Does the mood change radically from calm to angry? Does he or she ever threaten you with object or weapons? Does he or she ever give you visible injuries, such as welts, bruises, cuts, or lumps on your body? and have you ever had to seek professional aid for any injury at a medical clinic, hospital emergency room or doctor's office. Does he or she ever hurt you sexually or make you have intercourse against your will? ***The book of Job 5:21.*** If you answered **YES** to any of the questions, you may be living in an abusive relationship. The violence will not go away it will get worst, I and many others were fortunate to survivor and get out alive, but many are death and if you don't want this to happen to you or anyone who is facing the issue of domestic violence start seriously thinking about a safety plan for you or if children are involved.

How can pastors help in the church?

Pastors can listen to the victim, stand with her or him, and believe what she or he is reporting. Reassure them that the abuse is not their fault. They are not to blame, and what the abuser has done is wrong, even illegal. Reassure them of God's love and that God does not want them to remain in a situation where their life and the lives of their children are in danger. Pastors help the victim take inventory of the situation, assess the level of harm and danger involved. Be genuinely concern about any injuries she or he may have on the body, does she or he need medical assistance? Be patient in listening and allowing the victim the time to process her story. A Pastor's mission and first obligation is the duty of a prophet, to observe evil in our society and to speak out against violence by applying the Word of God in all situations. In the Bible, one of features most strongly emphasized for godly homes are safety. In the Book of **Psalms chapter 3 and verse 6 it reads: "I will not be afraid of ten thousand of the people that have set themselves against me around about."** Pastors make your church a safe place where abused women and abused men can come for help. Provide informative lectures on domestic violence in your church. Discuss with the church leaders, pastoral care, social justice committee, how the church can implement changes to ensure you reach those experiencing domestic violence. Faith leader, do you have a staff person who is willing to receive in-depth training on domestic violence. If you are interested visit F.O.C.U.S Ministry in Chicago Illinois where I was trained that provides training on domestic violence to all church ministers, priest, deacons and lay ministers. Dedicate at least one weekend a month to inform your congregation about domestic violence during the month of October, we all can heighten awareness about psychological abuse and gas lighting and teach people how to communicate without violence in a relationship. Remember, just a mention of domestic violence lets abused victims know that someone cares. In churches reconciliation services are good ways to help identify violence against women intercession for victims of abuse. Keep in mind that the church is available to help anyone experiencing violence in their home and relationship Jesus entrusted us to offer healing when it is needed. Domestic violence is an imposter in the church, whether pastors want to accept it or not believe it is prevalent and many attending services need help. The complexity of approaching domestic violence in the church is that male leadership are the key decision makers when it comes to church priorities and are far less active on the topic of domestic violence. Meanwhile, abuse by men, including men of the clergy has gone unchallenged and is under reported. Survivors also report a lack of training in how to respond to domestic abuse when it is in the churches. 1 in 4 women and 1 in 7 men have experienced domestic violence in a congregation, you could have more than a dozen women and half a dozen men who are victims and their abusers are praying right next to them. One of the greatest tools in healing from domestic violence is realizing that when you open the wisdom of your heart that was wounded your soul begins to align within the mind, body and being.Wounds2Wisdom llC was birth into existence as a testament to the creative power that the Lord anointed me with to give back to the world and not hold on to it because it never belonged to me in the first place. Wounds2Wisdom is a one-of-a-kind gift basket business to heighten awareness and embracing the opulent beauty aromatic scented candles, enchanting body cream, heavenly body shower gel that will make any bathroom a magical spa. A colorful brochure on nine ways to help those who are experiencing domestic violence, and a thank you card for purchasing, is our way to continue the fight in domestic violence.

Studies have proven the traditional definition of domestic violence is wife beating. Interesting, in 1929, the UCR was created to track violent crime reported to law enforcement, but it does not report domestic violence or sexually assaults. The UCR stands for Uniform Crime Reporting and collects information on crimes. Domestic Violence and Sexually Assaults are not part of that data base, therefore Wounds2Wisdom will continue in the efforts to enforce that domestic violence is a brutal crime with our gift basket. Reaching into households a life can and may be save from the hands of abusers. How can we say we are protecting our girls, boy, and people if we suppress the light one display in a relationship full of domestic violence? There is no way you can be great if you keep spitting out evil on the one you love, you are not great if you are dispelling evil words, thoughts, and deeds. Greatness is cherishing, embracing, laughing together, encouraging, and building each other up to a magical place that only the two of you share. In October 2023 the month of domestic violence awareness war of Humas attacked Israeli women, who were brutally burned, beheaded, rape, killed and kidnapped and had to remain silent due to the fear of a massacre on women. Those individual fell prey to the traps of the dark demons that belongs to domestic violence and no longer serves the country and themselves with LOVE. Despite those who does not want to report domestic violence in their data reporting, domestic violence is considered one of the most dangerous crimes in the world and tireless organizations, people, and churches all combined is still not enough. Awareness is a crucial step in stamping out domestic violence this is the only tool that will expose and erase this disease along with education and outreach. Readers when you hear about cases upon cases of battered women syndrome, ask yourself, do you agree that as a society we need better answers especially when the rights of individuals restricts our access to wealth, opportunities, and privileges in society to be free and not abuse.

Did you know?

Did you know that 4.9 billion dollars is spend on health-care expenses for Domestic Violence? This number indicates there is a global problem when it comes to domestic violence. We can never be sure of the outcome of abusers, but asking questions are a language for safety.

Did you know that The Universal church taught that slavery enjoyed the sanction of scripture throughout the antebellum period, many churches in the South committed version of the Christian faith with Black people believing that their version would help them to be good slaves and not challenge the slave system.

Did you know that Jesus was never afraid to confront we must confront domestic violence head on. Check out the following 100 sermons-sojo.net

Did you know The United States Department of Justice indicates a woman is sexually assaulted every two minutes. Approximately 28 percent of female sexual assault victims are raped by husbands or boyfriends, 35 percent by acquaintances, and 5 percent by other relatives. Nearly one-third of murdered women were killed by their current or former partner.

Did you know domestic violence accounted for 2983 homicides in 2021 alone. Children ages 17 and under are victims of 85 percent of all reported sexual assaults.

Did you Know that our former President Jimmy Carter established the office of Domestic Violence as a National Center for information in the year 1980 with a $900,000.00 budget for grants, research, and materials. One year later Ex president Ronald Reagan became President and that office CLOSED President Reagan stated due to the lack of funds.

Did you Know in 1971 the first women battered shelter opened in London was created. 1984 Television movie the Burning Bush highlight domestic violence. This book intricate details on how ancient laws legally acknowledged domestic violence as a homemade remedy to abuse women are immortal and unethical, therefore prayer is vital in connection for healing, but more must be done. We must have those sensitive and urgent conversation with our children, friends, relatives, and faith based leaders to keep the flame of domestic violence awareness high. It is so unsettling and destructive to go worship at a Holy place and must return to the abuser. The narrative is always safety and the question should be who is going to stop them, not who is going to let me know. Let's imagine for a moment, close your eyes, and imagine the walk through a shadowy aisle of wounded, broken hearted, fearful individuals with unspoken words unable to asked for help, what if a pastor in your church knew of this crime and did nothing and the next day individual is reported dead by the hands of a faithful tithe offering, likeable person. What will be your response in dealing with this tragic news? I am not judging all pastors or speaking of any situation, it is reality that these issues arise in the church and we must be prepared, Thus said the Lord. Unapologetic this topic is brimming full stream ahead and I have only touched the surface of how domestic violence is an imposter in the churches. I am ready to receive the good that will come out of reading this book and not pay attention to the negative views. Sadly, to say abuser's minds are warped demonstrating the terrifying power and control over a human being. The abuser who reads this book, my prayer is that you surrender your ill thinking warped mind to the truth of your innate soul and unlearned the violence of destroying others. Society has made tremendous changes over the past 40 years in the areas of domestic violence shelters, organizations fighting to terminate domestic violence in the lives of individuals, bringing more awareness and not giving up. However, domestic violence is still on the rise, and men especially are getting less sentences, decreased to misdemeanors or walking free after abusing their intimate partners. The tragedy of domestic violence is well-documented within police departments, counseling offices, and national organizations, but the one place it remains a secret and a source of denial is within the church. As a minister and student of the bible I saw women of various culture especially Christian women who lived with destructive relationships and reported the abuse to the law enforcement and little was done. The questions remain if love is the answer what is the question? The struggle is real for people who are verbally, emotionally, and spiritually abused by the ones who promised to cherish, respect, and love them. Some of these individuals use the cover of the church to hide their manipulative behaviors, with faith leaders requesting submission to the abuser. Submission will not solve the problem. Readers, in a survey provided by Lifeway Research pastors often don't know how to respond to victims, a great number of our leaders in the churches consider biblical text passages from the book of Ephesians 5:22, I Peter 3:1-6 and Titus 2: 3-5 to remind women to submit, to pray for their husbands, to be obedient, this may work well in a healthy relationship, but submission to an abuser give then license to abuse further. When the church affirms an abusive man's role as the head of the home, it gives carte blanche to men who need to be in control. In my 15 years of research and 7 years volunteering at Voices of Women Organizing Project working with the founder and powerful women survivors, I have heard over thousands of stories of domestic violence, but there is one woman story that touches my heart her story is so profound and compelling to how domestic violence change her life from pain to power. In my public speaking my prayer is that you will hear my story one day. To my sister survivors and those still trap in the dark web of a domestic violence, stay encourage with the following biblical scriptures.

Psalm 7:16 "His harm will return on his own head, and his violence will descend on the top of his own head.

Psalm 72:14 "He will rescue their life from oppression and violence, and their blood will be precious in his sight.

Proverbs 21:7 "The violence of the wicked will sweep them away, because they refuse to act with justice."

I pray that the book was a good read and nurturing to the soul, my closing message, I am sure many of you have questions as to why I am experiencing domestic violence in the faith? The book of Ezekiel 43:3 in its poignant message signals how our response to God greatness when forced with pressure, is up to us how me respond. Only each of us can answer the question as a victim or survivor of domestic violence when it shows up. Nevertheless, pray, stay connected with trusted people for support, ready the bible, find gratitude, and most of all have a safety plan to escape or get out.

Know your rights: Employment Rights of Domestic Violence.

Time off for medical care or mental health care, you have the rights under the Federal Family Medical Leave Act. It is illegal for any employer to take any adverse action against an employee who is a victim of a crime for taking time off to appear in court, consult with an attorney, or obtain a civil order.

Pursuant to NY Penal Law 215.14 under the Human Rights Law it is discriminatory to treat a victim of domestic violence any different than employees who need time off.

If you need to leave a job because of domestic violence you are not necessarily barred from receiving unemployment insurance benefits related to domestic violence.

Remembering the #Me Too Movement how the church was changed by offering help.

Love you. Stay strong and never allowed anything or anyone to take you to their dark world, your world is fill of light, believe it. Find a way to escape so that you reach your God given purpose. Minister Cheryl Prescott.

About The Author

Cheryl Prescott graduated in Theology Biblical Studies from the New York School of the Bible and was ordained as a minister in Queens, NY. She volunteered for seven years at Voices of Women, advocating for domestic violence awareness and implementing changes in the Bronx DA offices. Cheryl is also the founder of Wounds2Wisdom LLC, a business that supports domestic violence survivors through healing and creating gift baskets. She holds an Associate Degree in Human Services and works as an addiction counselor in Queens, NY.

www.ingramcontent.com/pod-product-compliance
Ingram Content Group UK Ltd.
Pitfield, Milton Keynes, MK11 3LW, UK
UKHW021024030225
454602UK00013B/841